Let's Use ADJECTIVES

MARIE ROESSER

Please visit our website, www.enslow.com. For a free color catalog of all our high-quality books, call toll free 1-800-398-2504 or fax 1-877-980-4454.

Library of Congress Cataloging-in-Publication Data
Names: Roesser, Marie, author.
Title: Let's use adjectives / Marie Roesser.
Description: New York : Enslow Publishing, [2023] | Series: Word world | Includes bibliographical references and index.
Identifiers: LCCN 2021042089 (print) | LCCN 2021042090 (ebook) | ISBN 9781978526969 (library binding) | ISBN 9781978526945 (paperback) | ISBN 9781978526952 (set) | ISBN 9781978526976 (ebook)
Subjects: LCSH: English language–Adjective–Juvenile literature.
Classification: LCC PE1241 .R64 2023 (print) | LCC PE1241 (ebook) | DDC 428.2–dc23/eng/20211122
LC record available at https://lccn.loc.gov/2021042089
LC ebook record available at https://lccn.loc.gov/2021042090

First Edition

Published in 2023 by
Enslow Publishing
29 E. 21st Street
New York, NY 10010

Copyright © 2023 Enslow Publishing

Designer: Katelyn Reynolds
Interior Layout: Rachel Rising
Editor: Therese Shea

Disclaimer: Portions of this work were originally authored by Kate Mikoley and published as *Let's Learn Adjectives!*. All new material this edition authored by Marie Roesser.

Photo credits: Cover, p. 1 LimitedFont/Shutterstock.com; Cover, pp. 1–24 iadams/Shutterstock.com; Cover, p. 1 Faberr Ink/Shutterstock.com; Cover, p. 3 Illerlok_xolms/Shutterstock.com; p. 5 Maros Bauer/Shutterstock.com; p. 5 botulinum21/Shutterstock.com; p. 5 Olesia Bilkei/Shutterstock.com; p. 7 Oleksandr Volchanskyi/Shutterstock.com; p. 9 Rasto SK/Shutterstock.com; p. 11 Africa Studio/Shutterstock.com; p. 13 lovelyday12/Shutterstock.com; p. 15 Ewelina W/Shutterstock.com; p. 17 VeKoAn/Shutterstock.com; p. 19 Evannovostro/Shutterstock.com; p. 21 Rido/Shutterstock.com.

All rights reserved. No part of this book may be reproduced in any form without permission in writing from the publisher, except by a reviewer.

Printed in the United States of America

Some of the images in this book illustrate individuals who are models. The depictions do not imply actual situations or events.

CPSIA compliance information: Batch #CSENS23: For further information contact Enslow Publishing, New York, New York, at 1-800-398-2504.

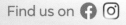

CONTENTS

Describe It!. 4
Nouns and Pronouns. 6
Sizes. 8
Colors 10
Numbers 12
Materials 14
Making Choices 16
Weather Words 18
Describe You!. 20
Glossary 22
Answer Key 22
For More Information 23
Index. 24

Words in the glossary appear in **bold** type the first time they are used in the text.

DESCRIBE IT!

Adjectives are special words. They tell us more about nouns and pronouns. They're often called **describing** words. Let's learn more about adjectives! The questions in this book will help. Be sure to check your answers on page 22.

QUICK

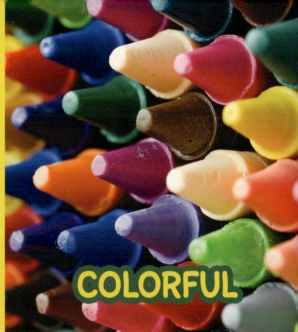

COLORFUL

TIRED

NOUNS AND PRONOUNS

A noun is a person, place, or thing. *Candy* is a noun. A pronoun is a word that **replaces** a noun. *It* could replace *candy*, for example. *She, I, you*, and *they* are more pronouns.

> Name the animal on the next page. That's a noun!

7

SIZES

How do adjectives tell us more about a noun or pronoun? An adjective could tell us the size of the building you live in. Is it a *tall* building? Does your mom work in the *tallest* building? Both *tall* and *tallest* are adjectives!

COLORS

Colors are another kind of adjective. Colors can help you tell **similar** things apart. For example, you likely have several shirts. You might say your **favorite** one is the *green* shirt.

> Which word best describe this fruit, *yellow* apples or *red* apples?

11

NUMBERS

Numbers aren't just for math! When numbers come before nouns, they're adjectives. They tell us how many of something. Birds have *two* wings, and butterflies have *four* wings.

> Does the plant on the next page have *one* leaf or *three* leaves?

MATERIALS

The **material** something is made of can be an adjective too. Imagine you ask a friend to play at your house. Help your friend find your house—with an adjective!

> Which adjective would you use to describe this house, *brick* or *wooden*?

MAKING CHOICES

Some adjectives are similar. Choose one that best describes the noun. A blue whale is the *largest* animal on Earth. It's not just *big*—it's *huge*! Imagine a whale next to the ladybug on the next page. You might describe the ladybug as *tiny*, not just *small*.

WEATHER WORDS

Weather can be described with adjectives too. *Cold, hot, windy, sunny*, and *cloudy* are examples of weather adjectives. People may use a few adjectives to describe the weather.

> Which weather adjective would you use to describe the sky on the next page, *sunny* or *cloudy*?

DESCRIBE YOU!

Adjectives describe you too! How are you feeling? Are you *happy*? That's an adjective. What **qualities** do you have? Are you *brave*, *funny*, and *kind*? Write down a list of adjectives to describe yourself. Aren't adjectives *awesome*?

GLOSSARY

describing Telling what something or someone is like.
favorite Most liked.
material Something used to make something, such as cloth or wood.
quality A feature of something or someone.
replace To take the place of something.
similar Almost the same.

ANSWER KEY

p. 6: cat
p. 10: red apples
p. 12: three leaves
p. 14: brick
p. 18: cloudy

FOR MORE INFORMATION

BOOKS
Dahl, Michael. *Adjectives Say "Incredible!"* North Mankato, MN: Picture Window Books, 2020.

Heinrichs, Ann. *Adjectives*. Mankato, MN: The Child's World, 2020.

WEBSITES

Adjectives
www.dkfindout.com/us/language-arts/adjectives/
Learn more about these describing words on this interactive page.

What Are Adjectives?
www.grammar-monster.com/lessons/adjectives.htm
Read much more about other types of adjectives here.

Publisher's note to educators and parents: Our editors have carefully reviewed these websites to ensure that they are suitable for students. Many websites change frequently, however, and we cannot guarantee that a site's future contents will continue to meet our high standards of quality and educational value. Be advised that students should be closely supervised whenever they access the internet.

INDEX

colors, 10

describing, 4, 10, 14, 16, 18, 20

materials, 14

nouns, 4, 6, 8, 12, 16

numbers, 12

pronouns, 4, 6, 8

qualities, 20

size, 8

weather, 18